MW00717330

From Life
To *Life*

Worship Services For
Lent and Easter

JOANN H. HARY

CSS Publishing Company, Inc., Lima, Ohio

FROM LIFE TO LIFE

Library of Congress Cataloging-in-Publication Data

Hary, Joann H.
   From life to life : worship services for the Lenten season and Easter Sunday / Joann H. Hary.
      p.   cm.
   ISBN 0-7880-0567-7 (pbk.)
   1. Lent. 2. Holy Week. 3. Easter. 4. Worship programs. 5. Sermons, American— Women authors. 6. United Methodist Church (U.S.)—Sermons. 7. Methodist Church—United States—Sermons. I. Title.
BV85.H384   1996
264—dc20   95-39876
                                                                      CIP

ISBN: 0-7880-0567-7   PRINTED IN U.S.A.

*To my husband **Robert A. Hary**,*
who is the first to hear all my sermons,
and who helps to stimulate new ideas
as we both work to serve our Lord!

To the Congregations
*of **Aurora United Methodist Church**, Aurora,*
*and **Grace United Methodist Church**, Lamont,*
who were next to hear these sermons
and who give me continual love and encouragement!

*With thanks to **Elaine Bliss***
who gave the manuscript careful reading
and attentiveness to technical matters!

Table Of Contents

Ash Wednesday
Order of Worship

The Gathering *(We gather in an informal candlelit room in a circle around a container where we can light a fire.)*

Words Of Focus On The Lenten Season
(Read quietly by one or several of the persons attending)

Greeting:
L: The grace of the Lord Jesus Christ be with you.
P: AND ALSO WITH YOU.
L: Bless the Lord, O my soul, and all that is within me, bless his holy name.
P: BLESS THE LORD, O MY SOUL, AND FORGET NOT ALL HIS BENEFITS.
L: Who forgives all our sins, and heals all our infirmities:
P: WHO REDEEMS OUR LIFE FROM THE GRAVE, AND CROWNS US WITH MERCY AND LOVING KINDNESS.

Opening Prayer:
L: Most holy God, your son came to save sinners; we come to this season of repentance, confessing our unworthiness, asking for new and honest hearts and the healing power of your forgiveness.
P: GRANT THIS THROUGH JESUS CHRIST, OUR LORD. AMEN

A Reading From Psalm 51:1-12

Response:
L: Cry, and God will answer.
P: CALL, AND THE LORD WILL SAY, "I AM HERE."

L: If you do away with the yoke, the clenched fist, the wicked word; if you give your bread to the hungry, and help the oppressed:
P: CALL, AND THE LORD WILL SAY, "I AM HERE."

L: Your light will rise in the darkness, and your shadows become like noon. The Lord will always guide you, giving relief in desert places.
P: CRY, AND THE LORD WILL ANSWER. CALL, AND GOD WILL SAY, "I AM HERE."

The Gospel Reading From Matthew 6:1-6, 16-21

Response:
L: May God have mercy upon us!
P: FOR WE KNOW OUR TRANSGRESSIONS, AND OUR SINS ARE EVER BEFORE US.

L: Behold, God desires truth in our innermost being.
P: MAY GOD THEREFORE PURGE US, WASH US, AND FILL US WITHIN.

Message: Invitation To The Observance Of Lenten Discipline

Time Of Silence And Meditation

The Bringing Forth Of Our Search Papers For Burning

The Burning

Thanksgiving Over The Ashes:
L: The Lord be with you.
P: AND ALSO WITH YOU.

L: Let us pray: Almighty God, you have created us out of the dust of the earth; grant that these ashes may be to us a sign of our mortality and penitence, so that we may remember that only by your gracious gift are we given everlasting life, through Jesus Christ our Lord.
P: AMEN

The Imposition of Ashes: *(Pastor uses the ashes from the burned papers to place the cross on the forehead of each person gathered.) As ashes are placed on each individual, the following is said:*

Pastor: Remember that you are dust, and to dust you shall return. Repent and believe the Gospel.
EACH: AMEN

Absolution:
L: In the name of Jesus Christ, you are forgiven!
P: IN THE NAME OF JESUS CHRIST, YOU ARE FORGIVEN!

L: Rejoicing in the fellowship of all the Saints, let us commend ourselves, one another, and our whole life to Christ, our Lord.
P: TO YOU, WE DEDICATE OURSELVES, O LORD! AMEN

The Peace:
L: The peace of the Lord be with you all.
P: THE PEACE OF THE LORD BE WITH YOU. AMEN

All may depart in quietness.

Words Of Focus

Note: *Signs have been posted at the entry asking all to enter in silence.*

The words of focus may be read by one person, but it is more effective if each paragraph is read by a different voice:

Genesis 3:19 gives us these words, "For dust you are, and to dust you shall return."

The room is darkened. We gather in quietness. We anticipate the ashes on our forehead and we wonder why it is that we have come here on this dark night.

Maybe it is because Lent is a time when we can be truly honest. We don't need to pretend. We don't need to cover up our feelings. We can let our pain be anguish, our aloneness be loneliness, our sadness be grief. There is something satisfying about entering into the suffering of Jesus.

When we go into the desert with him, we can feel the dryness of our lips, the parched feeling in our throats, the sun burning on our cheeks. We can hear the voice of the tempter and, knowing that it is the same voice that our Lord once heard, we look to Christ for strength.

As we solemnly turn our thoughts to prayer, we can see Jesus in the darkness of the Garden of Gethsemane, alone, as his disciples slept, and we know that he understands all anguish that has been caused by human rejection.

And when we think of his last days, the scourging, the crown of thorns, the slaps to the face, the purple robe, the mocking, and the shouts of "Crucify him," "Crucify him," and then his death on the cross, our own distress fades in the wretchedness of his suffering.

Oh Jesus, our Jesus! Your agony is healing balm for our struggles!

Lent: A time for healing! A time to give up our pain! A time of darkness that points us to the one true light.

1 Peter 2:22: "For it is by his wounds that you have been healed."

Ash Wednesday Message
Invitation To The
Observance Of Lenten Discipline

Dear Brothers and Sisters in Christ: Christians have always observed with great devotion the days of our Lord's passion and resurrection. It became a custom of the church to prepare for Easter by a season of penitence, fasting, and prayer. This season of forty days provided a time in which converts to the faith were prepared for baptism into the body of Christ. It was also a time when persons who had committed serious sins and had been separated from the community of faith were reconciled by penitence and forgiveness and restored into the fellowship of the community of the church. Even today the whole congregation is reminded of the mercy and forgiveness proclaimed in the Gospel of Jesus Christ and the need for all of us to renew our baptismal faith.

The central congregational action for us then is to examine our conscience: to search out particular sins, characteristics, or habits in our life that are hurtful or unjust. Not that this is any special kind of list, but rather, let the following be your starting point of thought:

- What have I done or said lately that makes me feel guilty or ashamed?
- How has selfishness interfered with my relationship with God, and with others?
- Of whom have I felt envious or jealous?
- How has false pride ruled my life?
- Of whom have I been intolerant?
- How have I been dealing with my anger?
- What resentments am I holding onto?
- Have I been feeling sorry for myself and expecting others to jump to my way of thinking?
- Have I been touchy, irritable, or had my feelings hurt very easily?
- What have I done that has been dishonest?
- What have I said that is dishonest?
- Am I careful not to start or pass on any rumors or gossip?
- Have I allowed fear to rule my life?
- What amends do I need to make?

You will be asked to write a word or two on a piece of paper which represents what it is that you wish to place before the Lord. You will then be asked to place that piece of paper in a common dish for burning in community with other believers. As we watch them burn away together, I pray that you will find new strength from God.

After the burning we will ask God to bless the ashes, and they will be placed as a cross either on your forehead or on your hand as a remembrance of the power of God's grace to restore and renew us as Christians.

I invite you now, in the name of the Lord, to observe Holy Lent by self-examination, penitence, prayer, fasting and alms-giving; and by reading and meditating on the Word of God. *(Small pieces of colored paper and pencils are passed around the circle.)*

To make a right beginning, and as a mark of our mortality, let us bow our heads and silently seek God to guide each one of us.

(Silent Prayer)

As you are led, write your words on the paper and bring them to the center and place them in a pile to be burned.

First Sunday In Lent
Order of Worship

Announcements, Prayer Concerns, Joys

The Lighting Of The Candles
Hymn: "Majesty, Worship His Majesty"

Call To Worship: (Psalm 130)
L: Out of the depths I cry unto you, O Lord;
P: O LORD, HEAR OUR VOICE.
L: I wait for the Lord, my soul waits ...
P: IN GOD'S WORD WE PUT OUR HOPE.
L: For with the Lord is unfailing love.
P: IN GOD, THERE IS FULL REDEMPTION.

Hymn: "God Of The Ages" (vv. 3 and 4)

Unison Prayer:
God of glory and mercy, when confronted by temptations, we are easily overcome. They allure us with promises we find hard to resist. We harbor fantasies of how our lives might have been. Our dreams become pervasive, hiding the truth of your love. O God, have mercy upon us; enable us to discern deception when it appears. Enlighten us to genuine renewal in Jesus Christ our Lord, in whose name we pray. Amen

Hearing God's Word
New Testament   Romans 5:12-19
Time With The Children

15

Gospel Lesson   Matthew 4:1-11
Sermon Text   Genesis 2:15-17, 3:1-7

Hymn: "Silence, Frenzied, Unclean Spirit"

Sermon: "That All-Pervasive Snake"

Responding To God's Word:
Psalm 32 *(Read responsively)*
Special Music: "I Am A Promise"
Silent Prayer
Pastoral Prayer
Lord's Prayer
Offertory
Doxology
Prayer Of Thanksgiving

Hymn: "Grace Greater Than Our Sin"

Benediction And Postlude
Recessional: "Shalom To You"

That All-
Pervasive Snake

*Introduction: In order to make this time of Lent come alive
for the congregation and to help us all to see ourselves in the
context of the Scripture Lesson, I left the pulpit, came to center
front and became some everyday characters tempted by Satan. Even the young children leaned in and paid attention as
the sermon came alive.*

Do you believe in original sin? If I asked, some of you might
answer quite cutely, "Yes, I believe in original sin, in fact I
have always thought that if I was going to sin, I might as well
be original about it."

Then, of course, there are the many stories, such as the
one about the church billboard that said, "If you desire to
be done with sin, come on in." As the people read more closely,
they discovered that someone had written in lipstick, "But if
you are not quite sure, call 555-5271."

What is original sin? Who is the tempter? Or temptress?
Is it really a snake? Does the devil still prowl around in this
world? Where does it all start? How does it get into our minds,

even when we are a very young age? You know, you tell your children not to go out in the street, and as soon as you turn your back, they have gone out in the street!

(Holding up a fake snake) I had bought this snake for our first Lenten symbol the other day when I went into town to do some hospital calls. My husband thought the snake as a symbol for Lent was a good idea, so he stopped yesterday at one of the department stores to get one for his two churches. He didn't find any in the toy aisle, so he was going to look at the fishing supplies to see if there would be anything there that would work. As he came up to that aisle, though, he also noticed some car mats that he thought he might purchase, so he went to look at them first. But as he passed the fishing aisle, he noticed a young boy, maybe 10 or 12 years old, sitting on the floor.

By the time my husband got back to the fishing aisle the boy was gone, but he caused a great calamity. Suddenly as my husband stepped forward, all the fishing poles went falling down around him onto the floor. You see, the young boy had booby-trapped the fishing equipment with a fine piece of fishing string. "Where did he get such an idea?" we might ask. "Is the devil at work inside his head?"

Lest we quickly decide that the devil only works inside the minds of children, let's take a look at the following vignettes to shed some light on how temptation works: *(Assuming the character for each)*

1. "Wow, I have really studied hard for this test! I spent hours and hours and have read the whole unit three times, besides writing all the answers to the questions. I have written imaginary test questions and answered them. I really feel good about this. But wait, I didn't expect *that* question. What's wrong with this teacher? Doesn't he know how to make up a test?"

ENTER THE SNAKE: "Why don't you sneak a quick peek over on Kelli's paper? Kelli always gets good grades. I know you have been told forever and ever that it is never right to cheat, but this time is different. You really studied. You don't deserve a bad grade. Why, just look, even the teacher doesn't care if you cheat. He just stepped out of the room. Go ahead. It will be okay.''

2. "The prom is coming soon. I am so excited! I can hardly wait. I wonder whether that gorgeous wrestler is ever going to get around to asking me to go with him. I can't wait to go with my mom to get my prom dress. That is always such a fun day. All those beautiful dresses! I remember last year and how good it felt to be all dressed up. Of course I think I have gained a little weight and I'll probably not be able to get into the same size dress as last year ...."

ENTER THE SNAKE: "Why don't you go on one of those crash diets like some of the other girls? I know Coach said to remember to eat lots of vitamins and minerals and proteins and carbohydrates to get ready for track, but what's a few weeks of starving? Think how great you will look, and on your birthday you can still eat your birthday cake. You can always just stick your finger down your throat and gag yourself. It's no big deal.''

3. "I'm so glad I got this new job. It is really wonderful to have some money to do the things that I want to do. Besides that, I like meeting all these people. It feels so good to finally have responsibility for myself. I am surely glad that I spent all that time in college getting ready for this. It truly is wonderful.''

ENTER THE SNAKE: "Aw, come on, you don't have to get up so early this morning. The boss said that you need to be on time every day, but it will be okay to be late. He really didn't mean it when he said that promptness is important. After all, he was late yesterday. And one day last week Jesse was late, and Jesse has been around the company for a long time and never got fired.''

4. "I'm glad that I finally got all my records together so that I can get my income tax done. It really does take a lot of time to get them all collected, but now that I have them all in a box and sorted it feels pretty good.''

ENTER THE SNAKE: "You know, you could just as well not take some of those records with you to the tax-preparer. After all, Uncle Sam will never know whether you earned a few dollars here and there doing sewing, or that you have been cleaning that big building across the street for petty cash, or that you gained a big profit on the land you sold. Why, you hardly make enough to live on now, without giving a percentage of it to the government."

5. Last One! "I have really been feeling good since the doctor finally got my insulin regulated. I really thought it was going to be awful adjusting to being a diabetic, but it hasn't been so bad. My spouse has been so wonderful, too, helping me to eat right. And they have come out with some great-tasting diabetic recipes and helps ..."

ENTER THE SNAKE: "You mean you aren't going to eat that scrumptious-looking piece of pie? The doctor never told you that a piece of pie would kill you, did he? Aw, come on, just taste it. It's just like a cloud. It melts in your mouth. Something that looks that good couldn't possibly be that bad."

And the temptations go on. Just as the snake tempted Adam and Eve beyond the breaking point, so also the tempter is there today. It may even be in the form of a so-called friend. It may be your own mind. It may simply be an attractive sign or commercial, or it might even be a basic need that is clamoring to be filled. Temptations come in all sizes, shapes and ways. For some, temptation comes when they are feeling down and just need a little "pick-me-up." For others, temptations are a part of celebrating something. Still others fall into the "Everyone Else Is Doing It!" trap. There are so many ways that temptations come, and there is no possible way of living a life that will avoid that happening. It has been that way since the beginning of time.

And the sad part is that it is oftentimes so unrecognizable. IF Adam and Eve had known what was going to happen, they certainly would not have tasted the apple .... IF the little child had known the pain of being hit by a car .... IF the youngster had known what a black eye and punch in the stomach felt like . . . . IF the test-taker had known how much it hurt to see that test being torn to bits and thrown into the wastepaper basket . . . . IF the teenager had known what bulimia would do . . . . IF that young person in his or her first job had only realized how easy it was to get fired . . . . IF the tax evader had known how easy it is to get caught . . . . IF ONLY, IF ONLY, IF ONLY . . . . And yet "IF ONLY" is a poor excuse, because isn't it the truth that, in most cases, we really do know what the "IF ONLY" is? Yet we succumb to temptation anyway. We know that IF we drink too much, we will be drunk. We know that IF we punch someone else, we are liable to get punched back. We know that when we cheat, we are likely to get caught. We know that when we put ourselves in dangerous situations, we will suffer the consequences. Yet somehow, just like Adam and Eve, we take a bite of the apple.

There is one thing for sure, when you hear someone spout, "What can I say, I am ONLY human!" they have probably yielded to temptation. And God knew that. That is why God sent Jesus Christ into this world. Jesus is the ONLY person who has been able to stand the test of temptation. By looking to him, we can gain two things. The first is how to hold fast when temptation comes. Our Matthew text tells us that when the devil tempted Jesus, he used Scripture to help fight the battle. And the second thing we gain is that through Jesus Christ we can be washed clean and set free even after we have yielded.

Recall the time that the crowd was ready to stone the woman who had been caught in adultery. They brought her to Jesus saying, "This woman was caught in adultery. The Law of Moses says she must be stoned." And Jesus said to the crowd, "Let that one among you who is without sin cast the first stone." And no one could even reach down to pick up a pebble. They all walked away, leaving her standing there with Jesus. And he said, "Where have they gone? Has no one condemned you? Then neither do I condemn you. Go and sin no more."

I want to close with a rather strange story from *The Upper Room* Daily Devotional: Canadian Stanley Baldwin tells of trying to bury garbage in his backyard when he was a college student rather than pay for garbage service. What no one had ever told him was that garbage service was free in that small college town. It took him a long time to discover that his digging and burying had all been just a lesson.

Similarly, many of us try to dispose of our garbage, that is, our sins and our shortcomings, in the wrong way. The good news is that God provides "Free Garbage Service" to every resident of his Kingdom, and when God gets rid of it, it is gone. Gone forever! Amen

Second Sunday In Lent
Order of Worship

Announcements, Prayer Concerns, Joys

The Lighting Of The Candles
Hymn: "Majesty, Worship His Majesty"

Call To Worship: (Psalm 121)
L: I will lift up mine eyes to the hills. From whence does our help come?
P: OUR HELP COMES FROM THE LORD WHO MADE HEAVEN AND EARTH.
L: The Lord will not let your foot be moved, the Lord who keeps us will not slumber.
P: THE LORD WILL KEEP US FROM ALL EVIL, AND WILL KEEP OUR GOING OUT AND COMING IN FROM THIS TIME ON AND EVERMORE.

Hymn: "Trust And Obey" (vv. 1 and 2)

Unison Prayer:
Holy God of Israel, you called Abraham to become the father of a great nation, and he responded faithfully. Grant us to know our own vocations and destinies in your plan, and that same kind of exceptional faith; that hearing your extraordinary promises for us, we may respond and find fulfillment, just as Abraham did. In Jesus' name we pray. Amen

Hearing God's Word
Sermon Text   Genesis 12:1-4a
Time With The Children
Gospel Lesson   John 3:1-17

Sermon: "But I Don't Wanna!"

Responding To God's Word:
Hymn: "Trust And Obey" (vv. 3 and 4)

Holy Communion

Offertory
Doxology
Prayer Of Thanksgiving

Hymn: "For The Bread Which You Have Broken"

Benediction And Postlude
Recessional: "Shalom To You"

But I
Don't Wanna!

"I don't wanna." "I just don't want to . . ." How many times have we responded to God in this way?

Let's do some supposing for just a minute. Suppose Abraham had said, "No, God, I don't wanna do that . . . I want to stay right where I am. I like it here. The soil is good and my family is happy. No, God, I don't want to be your Father of the Nations." Suppose Moses had said, "No, God, I don't want to help those people out of Egypt. They got themselves into the mess. They can get themselves out." Or just suppose Mary had said, "No, God, I don't want to have a baby. I would really be embarrassed." Or suppose Joseph had said, "Are you kidding? I don't want to have anything to do with a child that certainly isn't mine . . ." Or just suppose Jesus had said, "No thanks, God, I don't see why I should die on the cross for all those other people out there."

Of course we never do those kinds of things, do we? Or then again, do we? Try these common occurrences. One is likely to fit you. Maybe even more.

And God said, "Be faithful and do your confirmation lesson tonight. And go talk to your friend in faith. You know you need to get that done." And that other side of your heart, the "But I don't wanna" side, says, "But I don't wanna do it tonight. I have this television program I want to watch, and besides that I am tired, and Sally or Melissa, or whatever his or her name is will be calling me later, and we have to get those plans made for after the game ..."

And God said, "You need to go visit Grandma. It is really lonely for her since she has been in the nursing home, and she needs you to talk to." And the other side of your heart, the "I don't wanna" side, says, "But I don't want to visit her. She doesn't even look like my grandma anymore. She doesn't seem the same since she's been sick and in the hospital. Besides that I hate that home. Sometimes it smells in there and I want to throw up. I don't understand why I can't have my old Grandma back, the one who gave me cookies and candy and always was there for me ..."

And God said, "You know, you really should go to Sunday school, administrative meeting, Bible study. (You fill in the blank.) The church needs you!" And that other side of your heart, that old "I don't wanna" side, says, "But I don't want to do that. Why, it is the same time as one of my very favorite television shows. I can't miss that. I'd have to make a special effort to be there; besides that I've already done all those things. Let someone else take their turn."

And God said, "I gave you the talent of singing, playing an instrument, reading a passage. Why don't you use it to glorify me?" And the other side of your heart, that "I don't wanna" side, says, "But I really can't sing that well. Susy can play a musical instrument better than I. And what if I goof it up? I don't want to take the chance."

And God said, "You need to be intentional about your prayers. It is good to always pray for others and their needs, and you know that they need your prayers right now." But that old "I don't wanna" side pops up and says, "But I don't want to pray for somebody else. It takes long enough to get my own needs and wants taken care of without bothering with somebody else. Besides that I'm really not very good at praying anyway, so what I say probably wouldn't make all that much difference."

And finally, Jesus said, "Go and make disciples of all nations . . ." And the "I don't wanna" side of us says, "I can't do that. Why, what if I say the wrong thing? What if I get the door slammed in my face, or what if they say I'm being pushy?"

And I say again to you, what if all of God's people had said, "But I don't wanna . . ."? Where would you and I be right now?

Let's look at our Old Testament lesson for this morning. The Lord says to Abram, "Leave your country, your people, and your father's household and go to the land that I will show you." Now just exactly how excited do you suppose Abram was to hear a message like this: "Leave your country, your people, your family and go someplace you have never been . . ."? I can't exactly imagine that he was jumping up and down for joy. And yet Scripture says, "So Abram left, as the Lord had told him." "Why?" we might ask. Why would Abram choose to be faithful to God? But maybe the truth is: the why is not important. What we need to concentrate on is that Abram did exactly what God asked him to do. He began the epic journey, walking hundreds of miles in obedience to God's call. Now we aren't talking here about a drive down to the local church to attend a meeting for an hour or two, or over to the neighbors to invite them to worship with us and coming back home again. We are talking about picking up everything we have and moving to Canaan, a land of great danger because of the people who lived there. And later when a great famine hit that land, the Lord directed Abram and his family on to the land of Egypt, and so on and so on. The story goes on and on as God uses Abram in many ways to touch people's lives.

But if you really want to discuss the "Why?" of all of this, perhaps we might. And the answer to the "Why?" is: because Abraham had faith in God. He had faith that God would guide him in his decision making. And Abraham's faith extended to trusting God enough to know that even though he himself did not know where he and his family were going, GOD DID! And that was really all that mattered.

How did Abraham know this? God had told him that he would bless him, and Abraham believed it.

And through Abraham, God has promised to bless each one of us. Just for a little bit, I want to talk about how each one of us is blessed. First of all, what does it mean to be blessed? When I think in terms of being blessed I think of God in Exodus saying, "You will be my people, and I will be your God." When I think in terms of being blessed, I think of God's promise to be with us. Those who have seen the stage version of *Fiddler On The Roof* surely had tears in their eyes, just as I did, as the Jewish peasants packed up their carts, singing mournfully, "We will find a new Anatevka, a new homeland, because after all, God will lead us. God will still be with us." It is a painful time when we have to give up something or someone that we love, and yet God is there to comfort us, and to guide us, and to lead us ever onward.

What does it mean to be blessed? Most of all, for us Christians today who believe in Jesus Christ as our Savior, it means that God loved us so much that *God sent his only begotten Son that whosoever believes in Him, should not perish but have everlasting life. For God sent not His son into the world to condemn the world, but that the world through Him might be saved.*

Perhaps as we continue our journey in life and the other side of our heart pokes through and says, "I don't wanna ..." we need to take a few moments to ponder where we would be if our Lord and Savior had said, "But I don't wanna. Let them take care of themselves. If they want to be sinners, then let them suffer the consequences." But Christ didn't do that. Instead Christ chose to die to save us. Let us, too, choose to be obedient. Amen

Some thoughts about FAITH ...

(These might be placed in the bulletin for each person to ponder.)

FAITH is the substance of things hoped for,
the evidence of things not seen ...

FAITH is the awareness of utter
helplessness without God.

Sometimes **FAITH** must learn a deeper rest,
and trust God's silence when God
does not speak.

FAITH grows in valleys.

Any trouble that is too small to take
to God in prayer is too small to worry about.

Be persuaded that what God has promised,
God will also perform!

We are not justified by works of the law,
but by **FAITH** in Jesus Christ.

The sheep in the arms of a shepherd looks only
into the shepherd's face, and not to the wolves
nearby seeking to harm it.

By grace, you are saved through **FAITH**;
and that not of yourselves: it is a gift of God —
not of works, lest anyone should boast ...

FAITH takes God at His word whatever He says.

If God be for us, who can be against us?

The test of our **FAITH** is our eagerness to proclaim the Good News.

The end of our **FAITH** is the salvation of our souls.

Announcements, Prayer Concerns, Joys

The Lighting Of The Candles
Hymn: "Majesty, Worship His Majesty"

Call To Worship: (Psalm 95)
L: O come, let us sing unto the Lord;
P: LET US MAKE A JOYFUL NOISE TO THE ROCK OF OUR SALVATION;
L: Let us come into God's presence with thanksgiving;
P: LET US MAKE A JOYFUL NOISE TO GOD WITH SONGS OF PRAISE!

Hymn: "Sing Praise To God Who Reigns Above"

Unison Prayer:
Holy God of Israel, you have put up with human unfaithfulness and complaining throughout history. Empower us with your Holy Spirit; that, trusting in you, we can open ourselves more fully to your will and thus live at peace with ourselves and with one another. In Jesus Christ's name we pray. Amen

Hearing God's Word
Old Testament Lesson	Exodus 17:1-7
Time With The Children	
Gospel Lesson	John 4:5-42

New Testament Lesson   Romans 5:1-11
Special Music: "Into My Heart"

Sermon: "What's So Good About Feeling Bad?"

Responding To God's Word:
Prayer Of Confession:
Most patient God, we confess with shame that, like the Israelites of old, we have tried and tested you and at times we have
wound up wandering aimlessly in a spiritual wilderness of our
own making. Forgive us, we pray; give us, by your grace, the
desire and ability to commit ourselves fully, and to entrust ourselves completely to you. And lead us finally into the promised
glory of your coming reign. In Jesus' name we pray. Amen

Hymn: "Rock Of Ages, Cleft For Me"

Silent Prayer
Pastoral Prayer
Lord's Prayer
Offertory
Doxology
Prayer Of Thanksgiving

Hymn: "Hymn Of Promise"

Benediction And Postlude
Recessional: "Shalom To You"

Lent 3 Message
Exodus 17:1-7

What's So Good
About Feeling Bad?

The other day as I was sitting outside the pre-surgical room at the hospital with nothing much to do but wait, I opened one of the multitude of magazines there and saw this wonderful cartoon. There were two witches on brooms flying through the air. You know how we picture witches to look. Well, one looked pretty happy while the other was obviously very upset as she complained to the other, "I told you before we started out today that it was going to rain. But no, you wouldn't listen to me, you and your Pollyana attitude that all will be all right. I knew all the time we should have left our brooms at the garage and taken the mops."

And then, as most of you know, I have been spending more than enough time in the dentist's office lately. There were magazines there, too. This time I picked up a health magazine. I read an article titled, "What's so good about feeling bad?" According to the author, pain ensures our survival. The article says studies show that people who are depressed about something are more able to assess life than those who are cheerful, and that feeling bad is also useful because guilt or fear often keeps us from doing wrong things. And finally, feeling bad about not receiving a desired promotion, for example, might be exactly the impetus we need to reassess our life goals and to move on to something which is better for us.

And then as I left there and was traveling up to the hospital and listening to the Christian radio station, Joni Earikson Tada came on. There I was, sitting outside the hospital glued to the radio as Joni was saying, "The weaker we feel, the harder we lean on Christ. If we never were hurting, how would we ever learn to trust and obey? We would think we could make it on our own and our relationship with God would fall by the wayside." And those of you who know who Joni is know that this belief did not come for her at a small price. She was the victim of a diving accident that left her paralyzed. She lives in a wheelchair, and proclaims the love of Jesus Christ in every way she can, even by painting with a paint brush held in her mouth.

So often as I am working on a sermon, the most perfect examples surface during the week; but even scarier than that, so often what the humans in the Scripture that week are doing, so also am I. That, too, happened as I was hurt and humiliated by an incident where I really felt used, and it didn't take me very long to start complaining.

This all leads us into our Scripture lesson from Exodus: you know, that one all about the complaining Israelites! "What more could they possibly want?" we might wonder. God has been so physically active in their lives. Surely they ought to know that God is still with them. The Israelites have survived the many plagues that God sent to the Egyptians to cause the Pharaoh to let them go. They were right there to experience the parting of the Red Sea by God that let them walk through on dry land. God had sent a cloud which led them each day, and a pillar of fire to guide them at night; and they had Moses as their leader. And yet they complained!

Oh, this wasn't the first time, though. Just a little earlier God had to send manna because they complained of having nothing to eat. Then they complained about not having meat, so God sent them quail. And in our reading for today they are complaining and murmuring for water. One more time, God proves to them that he is still with them, caring for them and providing for their every need.

Of course, we aren't likely to do that, are we? Perhaps we are. As I already said, I did some complaining myself this week. So let us, just for a minute during this Lenten season, look at our complaining.

Do you remember a time when you moved, just like the Israelites? Maybe not as far, or as often, but most of us have moved at one time or another. We have been ever so grateful that we have everything all moved in, God has provided a home, and friends have been wonderful — and for just a little bit, we feel like we have it made. Then comes day after day of not being able to find what we are looking for, and we fuss and carry on, thinking a box must have been left behind, or some dummy carried it to the basement instead of the kitchen — well, you know how it goes . . .

God provides us with a beautiful, sunny day, no wind and it is as clear as can be, and we complain, "But it's so cold." Or we complain about needing rain and God sends one day of rain, and we are so happy we celebrate the rain. But then it rains a second day and a third, and soon we are so tired of rain we could scream. Then we start in again, "Why doesn't the sun ever shine anymore? I can't stand this gloomy stuff." Need I say more? I will!

We love going to school. Actually it is great to be learning new things every day. We enjoy seeing our friends. We love sports and the physical activity that keeps us pumped up. But let one teacher announce a test, and a big "UH" goes up in the room; and then let another teacher announce a test that day, too, and you'd think the whole world fell in on us. We start to complain about how much we have to do . . .

We listen to everyone else as they share programs for our women's group and we are inspired by their sharing and we are grateful. Yet when it comes our turn, we complain because we think we can't do as well as the person next to us, or it takes a lot of time, or the program that we are supposed to share seems so, so, so . . . well, you fill in the blank.

Our hearts keep on beating, our lives go on, our needs are provided for, and yet we complain about getting old, never mind where we would be if we didn't!

Complaining! It truly is a part of who we are as humans. But is the health magazine right? Is feeling "bad" good for us?

How often does the examination paper of life have a question we are so sure we can't answer, yet a few days later if someone asks us what we were so worried about, we can't even remember what it was?

Soon the robins will be back and they will one more time teach us a lesson that we so soon forget. We watch them as they peck in the ground seeking for worms, and they sometimes look despairingly down into the dead hole. And the robin decides to give up. There is nothing there. In fact, if he could talk, by now he would be complaining. But then it's like he suddenly has a second thought, and he pokes idly back into the hole. Suddenly the anticipation rises and before we can say "Poor Robin," he flies away with a juicy worm ...

The threshold of religion is at the point that the hungry soul, the hurting soul, the complaining soul stands squarely in front of the barren, hopeless situation, and realizes that it is only from God that the strength will come. It truly is as I quoted from Joni Earikson Tada earlier, "The weaker we feel, the harder we lean on Christ. If we never were hurting, how would we ever learn to trust and obey?" That, by the way, is something very similar to what my husband told me the other night after he had listened to my complaints for a while. I think it went something like, "Know that they spit on Jesus, and they didn't accept him, but he went on serving and loving, just the same."

How often do we demand proof from God in an instant, believing that God is supposed to show up like a genie in a bottle and make all things perfect with a "poof"? Why is it that somehow we think that God should make everything easy for us? That there is no price to pay for our personal spiritual healing? Do you suppose the Israelites really believed that they could travel all the way from Egypt to Canaan without any difficulties? Do we think that we should be able to travel daily down life's road without any struggle or pain?

Similarly, why is it that we tend to think that suffering means the absence of God? It surely didn't in the terror and pain of those hours on Good Friday. It was then that Christ chose to die for us without murmuring, and then rose again on Easter morning, even amongst our murmuring. God in Christ is the Rock, the rock of our Salvation. Oh, "Rock of Ages, Cleft for me. Let me hide myself in thee. Let the water and the blood, from thy wounded side which flowed, be of sin the double cure; save from wrath and make me pure!" Amen

Fourth Sunday In Lent
Order of Worship

Announcements, Prayer Concerns, Joys

The Lighting Of The Candles
Hymn: "Praise To The Lord, The Almighty" (vv. 1 and 2)

Call To Worship:
L: O come, let us worship and bow down!
P: LET US KNEEL TO THE GOD OF OUR SALVATION!
L: For God is ours!
P: AND WE ARE GOD'S!

Hymn: "Praise To The Lord, The Almighty" (vv. 3 and 4)

Unison Prayer:
Most Holy God, you have the power to see into our souls and to know our true spirits. Bring us to a better knowledge of ourselves: that, our illusions and delusions dispelled, we may know our shortcomings and open ourselves to your salvation in Christ Jesus, in whose name we pray. Amen

Hearing God's Word
New Testament   Ephesians 5:8-14
Time With The Children
Gospel Lesson   John 9:1-41
Gloria Patri
Sermon Text   1 Samuel 16:1-13

Sermon: "When Drudgery Becomes Joy"

Responding To God's Word:
Hymn: "Open My Eyes, That I May See"

Psalm 23 *(Read responsively)*
Silent Prayer
Pastoral Prayer
Lord's Prayer
Offertory
Doxology
Prayer Of Thanksgiving

Hymn: "Hymn Of Promise"

Benediction And Postlude
Recessional: "Shalom To You"

Lent 4 Message
1 Samuel 16:1-13

When Drudgery Becomes Joy

(We have a young boy named Kevin in our congregation who has suffered from cancer, and with all the treatments leading up to stopping the cancer, the family had spent not just days or months in the hospital, but years.)

Thursday as Debbie was waiting for a call from the doctor at Mayo Clinic as to what to do (since Kevin was again running a high fever) she called me to tell me that they were probably headed for Rochester. As she talked she said, "You know, we have all these doctors all over the place, and they are all good, but the very best one is still our own family doctor. He really knew what he was doing when he sent us home for the night. Our family had a chance to eat supper together; Kevin got to get out and run around, to play with Joshua (the dog), and to go out and see the cattle with his uncle before we'd have to go back up to the hospital at Rochester."

And then Deb went on to tell me how excited she was to be able to do the wash and some of the other things which needed to be done around the house. We discussed how interesting it is that she was finding this task of doing the wash something fun to do, rather than something she had to do!

Isn't it true that sometimes when we do things on a daily basis we just get tired of doing them? They aren't as much fun or rewarding as they once were, and we wish sometimes that we could just quit doing the wash, or cooking the meals, or shoveling the sidewalk, or feeding the cattle, just for a day or so, or maybe a week. Somehow, at times things become a drudgery rather than a privilege, and we grudgingly accept our responsibility, rather than remembering our call.

Perhaps that is the way it was for Saul. God had chosen him to be the first king and he really had accomplished much. He had defeated the Amalekites. He had engaged the fearsome Philistines in at least three major military battles, yet he wasn't really doing what God had called him to do.

But maybe before we go any further we need to back up and see how this all came about. Other nations around the Israelites had kings to lead them, so somehow they got the idea into their heads that they, too, needed a king. That really scared Samuel, because he believed that God should be Israel's one and only king, or otherwise suddenly the people might come to depend upon an earthly monarch rather than upon God. But the people were insistent, so finally, after much discussion with God about this, Saul, a man of great courage, size and skill as a warrior, was anointed — and what Samuel had feared did happen. Saul, human that he was, turned selfish and ruthless, and somehow forgot that *he* was holding a sacred office, that *he* was God's servant, and that *he* needed to do what God commanded.

In other words, his kingship became something that he had done rather than a privilege given to him by God, and he either grudgingly did the things he had to do, or just plain didn't do them at all, rather than remembering his call.

Well, of course, that did not please God very much, and so he decided to replace Saul with a new king. God told Samuel to find a new king. And here it is that Samuel begins to wonder about the work that God has given him to do, and he says, "How can I go do that? Saul will kill me!"

It is a scary thing to be one of God's elect, don't you think? But God chooses us more than we choose him. And just like Saul, and just like Samuel, we too have our excuses, "Thanks God, I'm touched by this honor, but no thanks!"

After all, "I don't speak very well. How can I be the one that God has chosen to talk to my neighbor about God?"

Or, "Why would you want to choose me, God? Don't you know how many sins I have committed? Surely I'm not good enough. How could I ever be an example of Christian living?"

"But you know, God, I am just a kid and I really don't know Scripture very well. What if they ask me a question that I can't answer?"

And God has heard all of those excuses before. After all, wasn't it Moses who said, "I cannot speak for you, I am slow in speech and of tongue"?

And young Jeremiah who said, "I can't speak for you, God, I am just a child."

And Jonah ran from God as fast as he could go, saying, "I cannot represent you, God, because I don't understand how you can be so merciful to those people who surely don't deserve it."

And then there was Zacchaeus way up in the tree, who never would have dreamt for a minute that he was worthy of having Jesus come to his house.

Or Peter, who finally said, "Just leave me alone, Jesus, for I am a sinful man!"

But the secret of election as God's servants is that God chooses us. God chooses us, not because of what we can do for him, but because of what he can do with us and in us and through us. And then the secret of our selection is in our willingness to stay open and willingness to listen to his commands, when it is often so much easier to do what we want, or even to follow what the devil says.

Let's look back again at our text for this morning. Saul in his humanness, selfishness and ruthlessness somehow forgot that he was holding a sacred office, that he was God's servant, and needed to do what God commanded. It didn't take very long before God replaced him with a new king.

And then, let's look at what happened with Samuel. After he questioned God, saying, "How can I go do that? Saul will kill me!" Samuel stayed around to listen to God, and God told him the way. God said, "Take a heifer with you and tell Jesse that you have come to make a sacrifice to the Lord." And Samuel did what God had instructed. Though he arrived in Bethlehem trembling with fear for what might happen, when he did just as God commanded, he was invited in by Jesse and was allowed to do God's work, to anoint the new king, David.

When we make these two comparisons, it does make us wonder though, doesn't it? We might even ask, "Does God really just allow some people, like Saul, to fall out of his grace?" Or we might even say, "Is God vindictive, in that he chose to stop supporting Saul and changed his allegiance to a new king?" If we are looking at Saul from the perspective of his enemies, we might say, "Saul is simply getting what he deserves." Others might say, "Well, he brought it all on himself!" The perspective of a friend might be, "How could we help Saul to find his way back?"

You see, as the Lord tells Samuel, "Man looks on outward appearance, the Lord looks on the things of the heart." And it is what is in our hearts that makes all the difference. Jesus reminded us later in one of the parables that the absence of one spirit eventually brings on the presence of another, and if the things of God are not the things of our hearts, then what spirit will have its power in us?

When we look at today's Gospel Lesson, we can find that very same comparison: we see two kinds of people, the Pharisees who were searching for a way to condemn Christ, and who couldn't see the good that was done in the healing of the man who had been blind since birth; and, of course, the blind man himself who, even after being subjected to the questioning and insults of the Pharisees and being thrown out of the temple, still believed in Jesus Christ and fell down and worshipped him.

Perhaps our New Testament Lesson sums it all up best: "Live as children of light and find out what pleases the

Lord. Have nothing to do with the fruitless deeds of darkness. Wake up, O Sleeper, rise from the dead, and Christ will shine on you.''

You have heard before that Jesus doesn't choose us for our ability, but rather for our availability. Even then he doesn't ask us to do anything other than to be the best that we can be. When we have faith and trust in God, he will empower us to become his servants doing the work that he would have us do. Amen

Fifth Sunday In Lent
Order of Worship

Announcements, Prayer Concerns, Joys

The Lighting Of The Candles
Hymn: "And Are We Yet Alive" (vv. 1, 2, 3)

Call To Worship: (Psalm 130)
L: Out of the depths, I cry to you, O Lord. Lord, hear my voice;
P: LET YOUR EARS BE ATTENTIVE TO MY SUPPLICATIONS!
L: If you, O Lord, should mark iniquities, Lord, who could stand?
P: BUT THERE IS FORGIVENESS WITH YOU, SO THAT YOU MAY BE REVERED.
L: I wait for the Lord, my soul waits, and in His Word I hope;
P: MY SOUL WAITS FOR THE LORD MORE THAN THOSE WHO WATCH FOR MORNING.
L: O Israel, hope is in the Lord
P: FOR WITH THE LORD IS STEADFAST LOVE!

Hymn: "And Are We Yet Alive" (vv. 4, 5, 6)

Unison Prayer:
God of our yesterdays, our todays, and our tomorrows, we are prone to live for the moment. You offer us the spirit to bring us wholeness, but we resist and often are overtaken by events; then we sink into despair. From the depths, you raise

us, if we cry out to you; but at times it seems we prefer sullen silence. Forgive self-pity that closes you out. We pray in the name of Jesus Christ. Amen

Hearing God's Word

Old Testament	Ezekiel 37:1-14
Time With The Children	
Gospel Lesson	John 11:1-45
Gloria Patri	
New Testament Lesson	Ephesians 5:8-14

Sermon: "Hard Times May Drop In For A Visit, BUT..."
  Hymn: "Dem Bones"
  Hymn: "Hymn Of Promise"

Responding To God's Word:
Silent Prayer
Pastoral Prayer
Lord's Prayer
Offertory
Doxology
Prayer Of Thanksgiving

Hymn: "In The Cross Of Christ I Glory"

Benediction And Postlude
Recessional: "Shalom To You"

Hard Times May Drop
In For A Visit, BUT . . .

I don't know how many of you have seen the movie *Sister Act*, but if you haven't, you probably should. It is filled with good humor, but it also makes a marvelous point. In the movie a casino singer witnesses a gangster execution and then agrees to testify. In order to protect this "wild woman of the world," the police hustle her off to an inner-city convent in San Francisco to pose as a nun so they can keep her hidden and safe until the trial. In the first place, she doesn't want to be there and keeps trying to get out, and in the second place, obviously, she just doesn't fit in with the real sisters that are a part of the convent.

She talks at the wrong time, fails to get up when she is supposed to, and gets herself into all kinds of trouble. And finally, not knowing what to do with her, they send her to practice with the choir. Now I couldn't imagine any choir being as bad as this one was portrayed. And come to find out, the singing was quite typical of the run-down condition of everything in the place. It was old, and dirty, and shut off from the world that surrounded it. The church that was part of the convent was as empty as the hollow singing that was going on inside.

It didn't take long until this atypical nun had that convent rocking and reeling, and singing and swaying, and the church began to fill up with people. The doors were unbarred, the windows were opened, and the convent became the center of life for the community. There was a breath of fresh air blowing.

The place that had been a valley of the bones, where all hope was lost, became alive and thriving, something like the song, "Dem Bones." Let's have a little fun, and try singing that right now. It matters not that we sound like a choir here, but rather that we try to get the message ... *(Sing "Dem Bones")*

"Dem Bones" was a vision of Ezekiel, and I want you to hang onto the word "vision," because Ezekiel did not actually have this happen to him; rather, God gave Ezekiel a vision so that he might be able to help God's chosen people through a rough period in their lives. Let me remind you about that time for God's people.

Let's start back about 10-12 years before this time, or 597 BCE. The Assyrian army, who had been holding God's people in Judah in a vassal state, collapsed to the stronger Babylonian forces. The Babylonians appointed Zedekiah as king.

The next ten years were a period of international intrigue. Nebuchadnezzar's army came down upon the walls of Jerusalem more than once before they finally laid siege for a period of over two years, eventually destroying everything in the year 587 BCE. Nothing was left. The walls were leveled, the city burned. The temple was plundered. Leading citizens were executed and others were carried off to exile in Babylon. Zedekiah, the king, was apprehended in flight and forced to witness the execution of his family. Then, in order to fix that terrifying sight in his mind, they blinded him and carried him off to Babylon, where he died.

It seemed that for God's people the glory had departed. They were defeated, degraded, dejected, humiliated, broken, plundered and sent into exile in a foreign land. Sometimes during Lent we use the symbol of an "instrument" to remember that they hung their lyres in the willow tree and sat down and wept. And if that wasn't bad enough, their Babylonian captors came along and required them to sing songs and told them to act as if they were happy.

Out of that pain they cried out to Ezekiel, "Behold, our bones are dried up, our hope is lost, we are clean cut off . . ." and, "How can we sing the Lord's songs in a foreign land?"

Now, get the picture: They weren't physically dead! They weren't bodies of bones scattered in the desert, but they felt like they would have been better off if they were dead! You see, Jerusalem had always been the place where Yahweh had caused his name to dwell, the place where they had always gone to give thanks to the Lord. Now their temple, their priests, the liturgies, and the place to sacrifice were destroyed, and they felt like they were clean cut off from God.

And they must have wondered why God would let this happen. After all, they were God's chosen people. "Was God too weak to protect them?" they wondered. "Or was God dead?"

Through Ezekiel God lets them know that they should not give up hope. After receiving the vision from God that said, "It is time to breathe new life into the people," Ezekiel encouraged them. He helped them make plans for a new temple, a new city, a new life. And with the coming of Cyrus some 50 or so years later the order was issued for the rebuilding of the Jerusalem temple.

Now notice that I said, "Some 50 or so years later." This was not an instant thing. Hope was not restored in a day, nor was Jerusalem rebuilt in a year. And yet so often we expect that to happen. Our life falls apart because of some happening, we become the valley of the dry bones, and we expect immediate answers. We get impatient and wonder where our God is.

We have all been through that, in one way or another. Perhaps the greatest hope we can have today comes from looking back on our own valleys of bones. When we realize that God has always been there, we then become more certain that God will continue to be there for us! For some of us we are talking about dry bones being "not getting what we really thought that we should have for Christmas''; for others, ''not having that very special person that we want to go to the prom with us''; and for some of us it has been the pain of divorce or the loss of a spouse. Still others have cried and cried when that last child left home, and they felt lost and lonely. I can remember how my mom was so down and depressed when my sister and her family announced that they would be moving a day's car ride away, and I can remember when a friend of mine was failing French class in college. You would have thought that the world was coming to an end!

Some of you out there have gone through a loss of your business or your family farm, had a pregnancy you were so hopeful about that ended in a miscarriage, gotten word that your son or daughter's marriage was in trouble, or have had a car accident claim the life of your best friend.

All of us have lived through those times, and we *have lived* through them. And as we lived through them, we cried out to God, wondering whether God was even there. And our bones felt dried out, cut off! In fact, even right now, there are probably broken hearts in many of these pews this morning.

But I also ask you, have you seen a tulip sprouting through? Have you seen a robin? Have you seen some geese flying back north? Is there some green grass in some of the warm spots of your lawn? Is not God's world full of promise, full of hope, full of renewal? Indeed, ''In the bulb, there is a flower, in the seed an apple tree, in cocoons a hidden promise, butterflies will soon be free. In the cold and snow of winter, there's a spring that waits to be, unrevealed until its season, something God alone can see.''

''Life with all its pressures and inequities, tears and trage-dies, can be lived on a level above the miseries,'' Chuck Swin-doll tells us in his book, *Come Before Winter*. ''If it can not, Christianity has little to offer and Jesus is reduced to nothing more than an apologetic beggar at the back door with his hat in his hands and a hard-luck story you can either take or leave.''

Don't believe that for even a moment. Because it is on the platform of pressure that our Lord does his best work, those times when tragedy joins hands with calamity, when Satan and a host of demons surround us and prompt us to doubt God's goodness. It is at such times that Christ silences the doubts and offers us hope to continue. In our Gospel Lesson for today we hear him say, "I am the resurrection and the life. He who believes in me will live even though he dies; and whoever lives and believes in me will never die."

"Though hard times may drop in for a visit," Swindoll reminds us in his book, "they won't stay for long when they realize that faith got there first, and doesn't plan to leave."

"In our end is our beginning; in our time, infinity; in our doubt, there is believing; in our life, eternity. In our death, a resurrection, at the last, a victory. Unrevealed until its season, something God alone can see." Let's sing it, "The Hymn Of Promise."

Palm/Passion Sunday
Order of Worship

Introduction: This worship service was dedicated to the sharing of Scripture. The reading(s) can easily be assigned to different people. In fact, in order to be creative and keep the attention of the congregation, we divided the reading so that characters were consistent throughout.

Announcements, Prayer Concerns, Joys

The Lighting Of The Candles
Hymn: "Hosanna, Loud Hosanna" (vv. 1 and 2)

Call To Worship: (The Palm Sunday Choice)
L: Jesus had a choice.
P: HIS WAS THE NOMINATION FOR KING IF HE WANTED IT!
L: But Jesus had other things to do.
P: PROCLAIMING GOD'S KINGDOM: TO SERVE INSTEAD OF BEING SERVED!
L: To rule the people's heart, not the government.
P: O JESUS, WE THANK YOU. YOU CHOSE NOT TO BE JUST ANOTHER KING.
L: But now, as on that first Palm Sunday,
P: YOU STILL PROCLAIM GOD'S KINGDOM OF SERVICE AND LOVE AND LEAD OUR WILLING HEARTS TO LIVE AND SHARE YOUR PEACE.

L: Hosanna to the Son of David, the King of Israel!
P: BLESSED IS HE WHO COMES IN THE NAME OF THE LORD. HOSANNA IN THE HIGHEST!

Hymn: "Mantos Y Palmas" *(Children enter waving palms)*

Unison Prayer:
L: The Lord be with you.
P: AND ALSO WITH YOU.
L: Let us pray
ALL: God our hope, today we joyfully acclaim Jesus our Messiah and King. Help us to honor him every day, so that we may enjoy his kingship in the New Jerusalem, where he reigns with you and the Holy Spirit forever and ever. Amen

Hearing God's Word
Proclamation Of The Entrance Into Jerusalem:
Gospel Lesson   Matthew 21:1-11

Hymn: "Hosanna, Loud Hosanna" (v. 3)

Prayer For Illumination:
ALL: God our redeemer, you sent your son to be born of a woman and to die for us on the cross; by your Holy Spirit, illumine our lives with your word, so as the scripture is read and proclaimed this day, we may be reconciled and won wholly to your will; through Jesus Christ our Lord. Amen

Old Testament Lesson   Isaiah 50:4-9a
Time With The Children
New Testament Lesson   Philippians 2:5-11

Hymn: "Jesus, Jesus, Jesus"

The Passion Story Proclaimed:
Matthew 26:14-29
Hymn: "O Master, Let Me Walk With Thee"

Matthew 26:30-56
Hymn: "Go To Dark Gethsemane"
Matthew 26:57-75
Hymn: "Ah, Holy Jesus"
Matthew 27:1-31
Hymn: "What Wondrous Love Is This?"
Matthew 27:32-44
Hymn: "O Sacred Head, Now Wounded"
Matthew 27:45-50
Hymn: " 'Tis Finished! The Messiah Dies"
Matthew 27:51-66
Hymn: "When I Survey The Wondrous Cross"

Responding To God's Word:
Silent Prayer
Pastoral Prayer
Lord's Prayer
Offertory
Doxology
ALL: No offering that we bring can compare, O God, with the offering of your son Jesus Christ, and the self-offering that he made on the cross. Nevertheless, may that example move us beyond giving to the genuine offering of ourselves in obedient service, at all costs, for Jesus' sake. Amen

Hymn: "Beneath The Cross Of Jesus"

Benediction And Postlude
Recessional: "Shalom To You"

Proclaiming The
Passion Story In Dialogue

The following speakers will be used: Narrator (N), Narrator 2 (N2), Judas, Disciple 1 (D1), Jesus, Disciple 2 (D2), Peter, Witness, High Priest, Crowd, Servant Girl, 2nd Girl, Bystander, Chief Priests, Pharisees, Pilate, Pilate's Wife, Soldiers. It would be most effective to have a different person for each role, but some could easily be doubled over, if necessary.

N: Then one of the twelve, the one called Judas Iscariot, went to the chief priests and asked:

Judas: "What are you willing to give me if I hand Jesus over to you?"

N: So they counted out for him thirty silver coins. From then on, Judas looked for an opportunity to hand Jesus over.

N2: On the first day of the Feast of Unleavened Bread, the disciples came to Jesus and asked:

D1: "Where do you want us to make preparations for you to eat the Passover?"

N: Jesus replied:

Jesus: "Go into the city to a certain man and tell him, 'The Teacher says: My appointed time is near. I am going to celebrate the Passover with my disciples at your house.' "

N2: So the disciples did as Jesus had directed them and prepared a passover.

N: When evening came, Jesus was reclining at the table with the twelve. And while they were eating, he said:

Jesus: "I tell you the truth, one of you will betray me."

N: They were sad and began to say to Him one after the other:

D1: "Surely not I, Lord?"

D2: "Surely not I, Lord?"

N2: Jesus replied:

Jesus: "The one who has dipped his hand into the bowl with me will betray me. The Son of Man will go just as it was written about Him. But woe to that man who betrays the Son of Man. It would be better for him if he had never been born."

N: Then Judas, the one who would betray Him, said,

Judas: "Surely not I, Rabbi?"

N2: Jesus answered:

Jesus: "Yes, it is you."

N: While they were eating, Jesus took bread, gave thanks and broke it, and gave it to His disciples, saying:

Jesus: "Take and eat; this is my body."

N2: Then He took the cup, gave thanks and offered it to them saying:

Jesus: "Drink from it, all of you. This is my blood of the covenant which is poured out for many for the forgiveness of sins. I tell you, I will not drink of this fruit of the vine from now until that day when I drink it anew with you in my Father's kingdom."

Hymn: "O Master, Let Me Walk With Thee"

N: When they had sung a hymn, they went to the Mount of Olives.

N2: Then Jesus told them:

Jesus: "This very night you will all fall away on account of me, for it is written: 'I will strike the shepherd, and the sheep of the flock will be scattered.' But after I have risen, I will go ahead of you into Galilee."

N: Peter replied:

Peter: "Even if all fall away on account of you, I never will."

N2: Jesus answered:

Jesus: "I will tell you the truth, this very night, before the rooster crows, you will disown me three times."

N: But Peter declared:

Peter: "Even if I have to die with you, I will never disown you."

N2: And all the other disciples said the same.

N: Then Jesus went with His disciples to a place called Gethsemane, and He said to them:

Jesus: "Sit here while I go over there and pray."

N2: He took Peter and the two sons of Zebedee along with Him, and He began to be sorrowful and troubled. Then He said to them:

Jesus: "My soul is overwhelmed with sorrow to the point of death. Stay here and keep watch with me."

N: Going a little farther, He fell with His face to the ground and prayed:

Jesus: "My Father, if it is possible, may this cup be taken from me. Yet not as I will, but as you will."

N2: Then He returned to His disciples and found them sleeping, and asked Peter:

Jesus: "Could you not watch with me for one hour? Watch and pray so that you will not fall into temptation. The spirit is willing, but the body is weak."

N: Jesus went away a second time and prayed:

Jesus: "My Father, if it is not possible for this cup to be taken away unless I drink it, may your will be done."

N2: When Jesus came back, He found them sleeping, because their eyes were heavy. So He left them and went away once more and prayed a third time, saying the same thing.

N: Then He returned to the disciples and said to them:

Jesus: "Are you still sleeping and resting? Look, the hour is near, and the Son of Man is betrayed into the hands of sinners. Rise, let us go! Here comes my betrayer."

N2: While He was still speaking, Judas, one of the Twelve, arrived. With him was a large crowd armed with swords and clubs, sent from the chief priests and the elders of the people.

N: Now the betrayer had arranged a signal with them:

Judas: "The one I kiss is the man; arrest Him."

N2: Going at once to Jesus, Judas said:

Judas: "Greetings, Rabbi!"

N: And Judas kissed Him.

N2: Jesus replied:

Jesus: "Friend, do what you came for."

N: Then the men stepped forward, seized Jesus and arrested Him.

N2: With that, one of Jesus' companions reached for his sword, drew it out and struck the servant of the high priest, cutting off his ear.

N: Jesus said to him:

Jesus: "Put your sword back in its place, for all who draw the sword will die by the sword. Do you think I can not call my Father, and He will at once put at my disposal more than twelve legions of angels? But how then should the Scriptures be fulfilled that say it must happen in this way?"

N2: Jesus turned to the crowd and said:

Jesus: "Am I leading a rebellion that you have come out with swords and clubs to capture me? Every day I sat in the temple courts teaching, and you did not arrest me. But this has all taken place that the writings of the prophets might be fulfilled."

N: Then all the disciples deserted Him and fled.

Hymn: "Go To Dark Gethsemane"

N2: Those who had arrested Jesus took Him to Caiaphas, the high priest, where the teachers of the law and the elders had assembled.

N: But Peter followed at a distance, right up to the courtyard of the high priest. He entered and sat down with the guards to see the outcome.

N2: The chief priests and the whole Sanhedrin were looking for false evidence against Jesus so that they could put Him to death.

N: But they did not find any, though many false witnesses came forward.

N2: Finally two came forward and declared:

Witness: "This fellow said, 'I am able to destroy the temple of God and rebuild it in three days.' "

N: Then the high priest stood up and said to Jesus:

High Priest: "Are you not going to answer? What is this testimony that these men are bringing against you?"

N2: But Jesus remained silent.

N: The high priest said to Him:

High Priest: "I charge you under oath by the living God: Tell us if you are the Christ, the Son of God."

N2: Jesus replied:

Jesus: "Yes, it is as you say. But I say to all of you: In the future you will see the Son of Man sitting at the right hand of the Mighty One and coming on the clouds of heaven."

N: Then the high priest tore his clothes and said:

High Priest: "He has spoken blasphemy! Why do we need any more witnesses? Look, now you have heard the blasphemy. What do you think?"

Crowd: "He is worthy of death."

N2: Then they spit in His face and struck Him with their fists.

N: Others slapped Him and said:

Crowd: "Prophesy to us, Christ. Who hit you?"

N2: Now Peter was sitting out in the courtyard, and a servant girl came to him saying:

Servant Girl: "You also were with Jesus of Galilee."

N: But he denied it before them all saying:

Peter: "I don't know what you're talking about."

N2: Then he went to the gateway, where another girl saw him and said to the people there:

2nd Girl: "This fellow was with Jesus of Nazareth."

N: Peter denied it again, with an oath, saying:

Peter: "I do not know the man!"

N: After a little while, those standing there went up to Peter and said:

Bystander: "Surely you are one of them, for your accent gives you away."

N2: Then he began to call curses on himself and he swore to them:

Peter: "I don't know the man!"

N: Immediately a rooster crowed. Then Peter remembered the words Jesus had spoken.

Jesus: "Before the rooster crows, you will disown me three times."

N2: And Peter went outside and wept bitterly.

Hymn: "Ah, Holy Jesus"

N: Early in the morning, all the chief priests and the elders of the people came to the decision to put Jesus to death.

N2: They bound Him, led Him away and handed Him over to Pilate, the governor.

N: When Judas, who had betrayed Jesus, saw that Jesus was condemned, he was seized with remorse and returned the thirty silver coins to the chief priests and the elders, saying,

Judas: "I have sinned, for I have betrayed innocent blood."

N2: The chief priests replied:

Chief Priests: "What's it to us? That's your responsibility."

N: So Judas threw the money into the temple and left.

N2: Then he went away and hanged himself.

N: The chief priests picked up the coins and said:

Chief Priests: "It is against the law to put this into the treasury, since it is blood money."

N2: So they decided to use the money to buy the potter's field as a burial place for foreigners.

N: That is why it has been called the Field of Blood to this day. Then what was spoken by Jeremiah the prophet was fulfilled:

N2: "They took the thirty silver coins, the price set on Him by the people of Israel, and they used them to buy the potter's field, as the Lord commanded me."

N: Meanwhile Jesus stood before the governor, and the governor asked him:

Pilate: "Are you the king of the Jews?"

N: Jesus replied:

Jesus: "Yes, it is as you say."

N2: When he was accused by the chief priests and the elders, he gave no answer. Then Pilate asked Him:

Pilate: "Don't you hear how many things they are accusing you of?"

N: But Jesus made no reply, not even to a single charge — to the great amazement of the governor.

N2: Now it was the governor's custom at the Feast to release a prisoner chosen by the crowd. At that time they had a notorious prisoner called Barabbas.

N: So when the crowd had gathered, Pilate asked them:

Pilate: "Which one do you want me to release to you: Barabbas, or Jesus, who is called Christ?"

N2: For Pilate knew it was out of envy that they had handed Jesus over to him.

N: While Pilate was sitting on the judge's seat, his wife sent him a message:

Pilate's Wife: "Don't have anything to do with that innocent man, for I have suffered a great deal today in a dream because of Him."

N2: But the chief priests and the elders persuaded the crowd to ask for Barabbas and to have Jesus executed, so when Pilate asked:

Pilate: "Which of the two do you want me to release to you?"

N: They answered:

Crowd: "Barabbas."

N2: Pilate asked:

Pilate: "What shall I do, then, with Jesus, who is called the Christ?"

Crowd: "Crucify Him! Crucify Him!"

Pilate: "Why? What crime has He committed?"

N2: Pilate asked. The crowd only grew louder:

Crowd: (louder) "Crucify Him! Crucify Him!"

N: When Pilate saw that he was getting nowhere, but that instead an uproar was starting, he took water and washed his hands in front of the crowd and said:

Pilate: "I am innocent of this man's blood. It is your responsibility!"

N2: All the people answered:

Crowd: "Let His blood be on us and on our children!"

N: Then Pilate released Barabbas to them. But he had Jesus flogged and handed over to be crucified.

N2: Then the governor's soldiers took Jesus into the Praetorium and gathered the whole company of soldiers around Him.

N: They stripped Jesus and put a scarlet robe on Him, and then wove a crown of thorns and set it on His head.

N2: They put a staff in His right hand and knelt in front of Him and mocked Him saying:

Soldiers: "Hail, King of the Jews!"

N: They spit on Jesus!

N2: And then they took the staff they had given Him, and struck Him on the head again and again.

N: When they had finished mocking Him they took off the robe and put His own clothes back on Him.

N2: Then they led Him away to be crucified.

Hymn: "What Wondrous Love Is This?"

N: As they were going out, they met a man from Cyrene, named Simon, and they forced him to carry the cross.

N2: They came to a place called Golgotha (which means The Place of the Skull).

N: There they offered Him wine to drink, mixed with gall; but after tasting it, He refused to drink it.

N2: When they had crucified Him, they divided up His clothes by casting lots.

N: And sitting down, they kept watch over Him. Above His head they placed the written charge against Him:

Soldiers: "This is Jesus, King of the Jews!"

N2: Two robbers were crucified with Him, one on His right, and one on His left.

N: Those who passed by hurled insults at Him, shaking their heads and saying:

Bystanders: "You who are going to destroy the temple and build it in three days, save yourself! Come down from the cross, if you are the Son of God!"

N2: In the same way the chief priests, the teachers of the law and the elders mocked Him, saying:

Chief Priests, Pharisees: *(Together or separately)* "He saved others, but He can't save Himself! He's the King of Israel. Let Him come down now from the cross, and we will believe in Him. He trusts in God. Let God rescue Him now if God wants Him, for He said, 'I am the Son of God.' "

N: In the same way, the robbers who were crucified with Him also heaped insults on Him.

Hymn: "O Sacred Head, Now Wounded"

N2: From the sixth hour until the ninth hour, darkness came over the land. About the ninth hour, Jesus cried out in a loud voice.

Jesus: *(Loudly)* "Eloi, Eloi, lama sabachthani!"

N: Which means:

Jesus: "My God, My God, why have you forsaken me?"

N2: When those standing by heard this they said:

Crowd: "He is calling Elijah!"

N: Immediately one of them ran and got a sponge. He filled it with wine vinegar, put it on a stick, and offered it to Jesus to drink.

N2: But the rest said:

Crowd: "Leave Him alone. Let's see if Elijah comes to save Him."

N: And when Jesus had cried out again in a loud voice, He gave up His Spirit.

Hymn: " 'Tis Finished! The Messiah Dies"

N2: At that moment the curtain of the temple was torn in two from top to bottom.

N: The earth shook and the rocks split.

N2: The tombs broke open and the bodies of many holy people who had died were raised to life. They came out of their tombs, and after Jesus' resurrection they went into the holy city and appeared to people.

N: When the centurion and those with Him who were guarding Jesus saw the earthquake and all that had happened they were terrified and exclaimed:

Soldiers: "Surely He was the Son of God!"

N2: Many women were there, watching from a distance. They had followed Jesus from Galilee to care for His needs.

N: Among them were Mary Magdalene, Mary, mother of James and Joseph, and the mother of the sons of Zebedee.

N2: As evening approached, there came a rich man from Arimathea, named Joseph, who had himself become a disciple of Jesus. Going to Pilate, he asked for Jesus' body, and Pilate ordered that it be given to him.

N: Joseph took the body, wrapped it in a clean linen cloth, and placed it in his own new tomb that he had cut out of the rock. He rolled a big stone in front of the entrance to the tomb and went away.

N2: Mary Magdalene and the other Mary were sitting there across from the tomb.

N: The next day, the one after the Preparation Day, the chief priests and the Pharisees went to Pilate and said:

Chief Priests, Pharisees: "Sir, we remember that while He was still alive that deceiver said, 'After three days, I will rise again.' So give the order for the tomb to be made secure until the third day. Otherwise His disciples may come and steal the body and tell the people that He has been raised from the dead. This last deception will be worse than the first."

N2: Pilate said to them:

Pilate: "Take a guard. Go and make the tomb as secure as you know how."

N: So they went and made the tomb secure by putting a seal on the stone and posting a guard.

Hymn: "When I Survey The Wondrous Cross"

Maundy Thursday
Order of Worship

The Gathering *(Congregation gathers together in the fellowship hall and sits at tables already prepared for the Seder Meal.)*

Announcements, Prayer Concerns, Joys

The Lighting Of The Candles
Hymn: "Kum Ba Yah"

The Passover Seder Haggadah

A Drama
(Any suitable drama may be performed, but the Seder Dinner is always the same. Performers might choose to gather once a week during Lent for devotions and rehearsal.

A CSS Publishing Company resource suitable for this event is *The Bread, The Cup, The Call And The Challenge* by Roger E. Loper, 1992.)

Holy Communion

Benediction

Maundy Thursday
The Passover
Seder Haggadah

(A 3,500-year-old worship service performed on the early nights of Passover week, adapted for easier understanding.)

The ladies light the festival candles at each table.

All sing "Kum Ba Yah"

Narrator — Introduction

Kadaysh
(Leaders fill each person's glass with juice.)

N: Please stand.

P: Blessed are you, O Lord our God, King of the universe, who created the fruit of the vine. Blessed are you, O Lord our God, who has chosen us for your service from among the nations, exalting us by making us holy through your commandments (Deuteronomy 7:6). In love you have given us, O Lord

our God, holidays for joy and festivals for gladness. You did give us this Feast of Unleavened Bread, the season of freedom, in commemoration of our liberation from Egypt. You have sanctified us by giving us, with love and gladness, your holy festival as a heritage. Blessed are you, O Lord, King of the universe, who has kept us in life, who has preserved us and enabled us to reach this season.

(Drink first glass of juice.)

N: Please be seated.

Urchatz
N: The second ceremony of the Seder is known as Urchatz, Washing of the Hands. This is a symbolic act of purification, which precedes our participation in this religious service.

(Narrator instructs; each leader washes hands.)

Karpas
N: The third ceremony is eating the Karpas. The Karpas is the celery. *(Take one piece of celery, and dip it into one of the three dishes of salt water on the table.)* We now dip this green fruit of the earth into salt water, as we recite together:

P: In partaking of this fruit of the earth, we give thanks to God for all his bounties. We also recall that our ancestors were farmers and were grateful for the earth's produce. In tasting the salt water, we remember the tears which they shed, while suffering the tortures of slavery. May our gratitude for the blessings convert tears to joy and appreciation. Blessed are you, O Lord our God, King of the universe, who created the fruit of the earth. *(The Karpas [celery] is now eaten.)*

Yachatz
N: We now perform the ceremony of Yachatz. We will now make the three pieces of Matzoh, by folding the Matzoh in

half and breaking out a large center circle. Break the center piece in half and lay to the side. Take the remaining Matzoh and break into two equal pieces so that one is the top and the other the bottom. The middle piece is the Afikomen, the dessert, to be eaten at the conclusion of our meal.

Mageed

N: *(Raises up the Matzoh and says)* This is the bread of affliction, the humble and simple bread which our ancestors ate in the land of Egypt. Let us join together at this Seder, and eat of what we have to share.

P: **With gratitude for the blessings that have been given, we invite all to share with us at this meal, and at other meals.**

N: May all God's people, wherever they are, those still deprived of total freedom, enjoy liberty at this time next year.

P: **May the people of the world speedily attain freedom from fear and want and be privileged to build a symbol of peace for all nations.**

N: Once we were slaves to Pharaoh in Egypt, and the Lord in his goodness and mercy brought us out from that land with a mighty hand and an outstretched arm.

P: **Had He not rescued us from the hand of the Pharaoh, surely we and our children would still be enslaved and deprived of human dignity.**

N: So we gather year after year to retell this story. It is a story which is ancient but eternal in its message and its spirit.

The Four Questions And Answers — Children (Youth leading)
C: *Why is this night different from all other nights? Why on all other nights do we eat either the Chametz (leavened bread) or Matzoh, but on this night we eat only Matzoh?*

76

N: We eat the Matzoh to remember that our ancestors, in their haste to leave Egypt, couldn't wait for bread to rise.

C: *Why on all other nights do we eat all kinds of herbs, but on this night we eat only Moror?*

P: We eat of the Moror on this night that we might taste of some bitterness, to remind ourselves how bitter life is for one who is a slave.

C: *Why on all other nights do we not dip at all, but on this night we dip twice?*

N: In the course of this service, we dip greens in salt water to replace tears with gratefulness, and Moror in Charoset to sweeten bitterness and suffering.

C: *Why on all other nights do we eat either sitting or reclining, but on this night we eat reclining?*

P: Tonight we pretend to recline because to recline at meal-times in ancient days was a sign of freedom. On this night of Passover, we demonstrate this feeling of complete freedom by imagining we are reclining throughout this whole meal.

The Lord's Promise
N: Blessed is God who fulfills his promises, who is ever faithful to his servants who trust in him.

P: The Lord foretold the events of Israel's bondage when telling Abraham about the future of his children.

N: Then God described the years of their service on foreign soil, tormented by strange and hostile people (Genesis 15:13).

P: God also promised to rescue and redeem them, bringing judgment upon the cruel oppressor (Genesis 15:14-16).

N: Great has been the Lord's divine promise, fulfilled and realized in days past.

(All raise their cups.)

N: In every age, oppressors rose against us to crush our spirits and bring us low.

P: From the hands of all these tyrants and conquerors the Lord rescued and restored His people.

N: Not in Egypt alone do God's people face the threat of complete destruction.

P: In many lands and many ages, God's people have faced the fierce winds of tyranny.

N: In all these battles and desperate struggles, God's help and guidance assured our survival.

P: Our hope and faith in God is strong, that no enemy shall ever defeat the people of God.

(Cups are put down.)

Ten Plagues
N: When Pharaoh wouldn't listen to the command of God to let his people go, he invited trouble upon himself and his people.

P: Though the plagues that came upon the Egyptians were a result of the Pharaoh's actions, we are not happy for their pain, because as children of God, we never seek to destroy others.

N: Since a full cup is the symbol of complete joy, a half-cup will express our sorrow over the losses caused by the plagues. *(Leaders fill each person's cup half-full.)* Listen and picture as I tell of the ten plagues: Blood, Frogs, Gnats, Flies, Beasts, Boils, Hail, Locusts, Darkness, Slaying of the Firstborn.

Dayenu

N: Great and numerous are the kindnesses which the Lord extended to our fathers. For each of them, we offer thanks and humble gratitude.

P: **Any one of these would have been sufficient to show his love for us.**

N: With great loving-kindness he redeemed us from Egypt.

P: **With awesome might he divided the Red Sea (Exodus 14:13-29).**

N: With tender care he protected us in the wilderness.

P: **For 40 years he provided for all our needs (Exodus 16:4-16).**

N: With abundant love he gave us the Sabbath (Exodus 16:22-30).

P: **At Mount Sinai he brought us the Ten Commandments (Exodus 19:1-23).**

N: In triumphant spirit, he led us into the Promised Land.

P: **For each act of goodness, we are abundantly grateful.**

Our Personal Deliverance — B'Chol

N: Every person must look upon himself or herself as though he or she, personally, was among those who went forth from Egypt. The events in Egypt delivered our ancestors, ourselves, and our families.

P: *(Raising our cups)* **We join now in praising and glorifying God's Holy Name. We are thankful. God delivered us from slavery to freedom, from sorrow to happiness, from mourning to rejoicing, from darkness to light. In gratitude, we shall sing songs of praise.** *(Sing "Praise God From Whom All Blessings Flow." The cups are put down.)*

79

Hallel
N: With renewed fervor, we give you thanks for our physical deliverance and our spiritual freedom.

P: Blessed are you, O Lord our God, King of the universe, who created the fruit of the vine. *(The half-cup of juice is drunk.)*

Rachatz
N: Before we eat the meal, we shall wash our hands, reciting the prescribed blessing. *(Leaders will wash their hands while the people recite):*

P: Blessed are you, O Lord our God, King of the universe, who has sanctified us by your commandments.

Motzee Matzah
(The leaders will break the piece of middle Matzoh and give to each person.)

P: Blessed are you, O Lord our God, King of the universe, who brings forth the bread from the earth and who sanctifies us by your commandments. *(The piece of Matzoh is eaten.)*

Moror
(Leader breaks the two pieces of Matzoh so that each person has a bottom and top piece. Each person places some Moror and Charoset between the two pieces of Matzoh.)

N: We shall now eat of the Moror, combined with the Charoset. In doing this, we remember how bitter is slavery, and how it can be sweetened by God's redemption. We recite together:

P: Blessed are you, O Lord our God, King of the universe, who has sanctified us by your commandments. *(Moror and Charoset on Matzoh is eaten.)*

Schulchan Oraych
N: In place of the full dinner we will now eat the Egg. *(Egg is eaten.)*

Tzofun

N: In ancient times, the Paschal Lamb was the last food to be eaten. "Afikomen" means dessert and the Lamb will be our dessert. *(All eat Lamb.)*

Boraych
(Juice glasses are filled.)
N: Let us pray.

P: Let us bless God's name forever and ever.

N: For everyone seated at these tables and for the food that we have eaten, we offer thanks to God.

P: We are grateful for the blessing of life, and for the privilege of enjoying the beauty and the goodness of the world around us. For all this we give thanks to you and praise you, O God.

N: We are about to partake of the third cup of juice, in gratitude for the freedom which the Lord granted our ancestors.

P: Blessed are you, O Lord our God, King of the universe, who created the fruit of the vine. *(Drink the juice.)*

The Earth's Bounties
(The leaders fill the juice glasses and glasses are raised.)

N: We now drink the fourth and final cup of juice as we recite together:

P: Blessed are you, O Lord our God, King of the universe, for the fruit of the vine, and for all the produce of the field. We give thanks to you for all your goodness to us and for all your loving-kindness. Blessed are you, O God. Amen *(Drink the last cup of juice.)*

Nirtzoh

N: This Passover Seder is now completed. It is time for us to share in Christ's Passover Seder. Children, there has been a piece of the Matzoh hidden which represents the Messiah. Search for it and bring it to the Lord's Table. *(After the children find the hidden Matzoh and return to their tables, a drama, such as, "The Bread, The Cup, The Call And The Challenge" by Roger Loper, may begin.)*

Good Friday
Order of Worship

Since this is an Ecumenical Service with all of the churches in the communities and their pastors involved, a drama such as "No Condemnation" from the book *Forsaken** by Robert E. Mitchell (published by CSS Publishing Co., Lima, Ohio, 1993) is a very meaningful choice. Other suitable dramas or readings may be used.

The Home Church provides a Lay Person to lead the congregation. The Visiting Churches provide a Lay Person to drive the nails, a Lay Person to light the candles, and a choir. The Pastors read the Dramatic Reading, "No Condemnation."

Welcome And Invocation
(Home Church Pastor)

The Tenebrae Drama
(including the following hymns in order of singing)
" 'Tis Finished! The Messiah Dies"
"O Sacred Head, Now Wounded"
"Were You There?"
"Ah, Holy Jesus"
"Go To Dark Gethsemane"
"What Wondrous Love Is This?"
"Alas, And Did My Savior Bleed"
"In The Cross Of Christ I Glory"
"Beneath The Cross Of Jesus"
"When I Survey The Wondrous Cross"
"Jesus, Keep Me Near The Cross"

*Contains the full Order of Worship and the Drama

Easter Sunday Sunrise Service
Order of Worship

The Youth Group of the church may perform a drama early on Easter morning. The drama titled, *We Love To Tell The Story**, an Easter Sunrise Service for Youth by Joann H. Hary (published by CSS Publishing Co., Lima, Ohio, 1994) is a scriptural choice. Other suitable dramas may be used.

*Contains the full Order of Worship and the Drama

Announcements, Prayer Concerns, Joys

The Lighting Of The Candles
Hymn: "Up From The Grave He Arose" (v. 1)

Call To Worship: (Psalm 118)
L: This is the day that the Lord has made!
P: LET US REJOICE AND BE GLAD IN IT!
L: God is our strength and our song.
P: GOD HAS BECOME OUR SALVATION.
L: We therefore will never die.
P: GOD HAS OPENED THE GATES OF RIGHT-
EOUSNESS!
L: Let us enter through them and give thanks!
P: LET US GIVE THANKS FOR GOD'S GOODNESS AND
STEADFAST LOVE!

Hymn: "Up From The Grave He Arose" (vv. 2 and 3)

Prayer:
L: It is good to give thanks to you, Lord ...
P: FOR YOUR LOVE ENDURES FOREVER!
L: We declare it with the House of Israel ...
P: FOR YOUR LOVE ENDURES FOREVER!

L: We declare it with the church of the Risen Christ ...
P: FOR YOUR LOVE ENDURES FOREVER!
L: We declare it with seeking disciples ...
P: FOR YOUR LOVE ENDURES FOREVER!
L: We declare it with the bereaved and dying ...
P: FOR YOUR LOVE ENDURES FOREVER!
ALL: IN JESUS CHRIST, CRUCIFIED AND RISEN!
AMEN

Hearing God's Word

First Lesson	Acts 10:34-43
Time With The Children	
Gospel Lesson	John 20:1-18
Gloria Patri	
New Testament	Colossians 3:1-4

Hymn: "Christ The Lord Is Risen Today"

Sermon: "Easter Celebration Is Just A Foretaste ..."

Responding To God's Word:
Hymn: "When We All Get To Heaven"

Offertory
Doxology
Prayer Of Thanksgiving

Holy Communion:
As you receive the elements today, the giver will say, "The body of our Risen Christ!" Your response will be "ALLELUIA." The giver will say: "The blood that saves!" Your response will be "AMEN!"

Hymn: "Because He Lives"

Benediction And Postlude

L: Christ is Risen!

P: CHRIST IS RISEN INDEED! ALLELUIA!

L: Go now, and may the peace of the Risen Christ go with you!

P: WE GO TO SPREAD THE GOOD NEWS. CHRIST IS RISEN AND IS LIVING IN OUR HEARTS!

Recessional: "Alleluia"

Easter Celebration Is Just A Foretaste . . .

Mark 8:31 has Jesus teaching his disciples that the Son of Man must suffer many things and be rejected by the chief priests and elders, and that he must be killed and *after three days* rise again.

Matthew 27:53 tells that the Pharisees went to Pilate saying that Jesus had told them, *"After three days* I will rise again."

In Luke 18:33, Jesus took the twelve aside and told them, "They will mock the Son of Man, spit on him, flog him, and kill him. *On the third day* he will rise again."

Yet isn't is strange that on Easter morning at the breaking of dawn, when Mary came to the tomb to anoint the body of Jesus, she reacted the way she did? She ran to tell Peter that the tomb was empty, not *that Jesus had risen,* but that the tomb was empty! And Peter and John, upon hearing the news, ran to the gravesite to see for themselves. They looked into the tomb, saw the burial clothes and the napkin for Jesus' head rolled up separately, and *it doesn't even seem that they remembered the words of Jesus that he would rise on the third day.*

"Why?" we wonder. Why do we have an accounting of these details about the fear of looking and the way the grave clothes are lying when seemingly they should have been excitedly sharing the news that Jesus had risen?

Perhaps the reason for these seemingly irrelevant details is that John is calling his readers to faith. John is calling his hearers to believe. And the call is to believe that Jesus Christ truly is the Son of God!

We started our Sunrise service this morning in the dark hours of death, with grief for the loss of a loved one, with an emptiness and loneliness like no other. That is truly where Easter must begin because it is in the darkness that the Great News of Easter meets us.

Actually Easter began a long, long time ago with an almighty and everlasting God who continues to love us all, even in the midst of our darkness. Easter continued for us as we faced the dark hours of Good Friday, and it burst forth in mystery and grandeur as God the Father glorified his Son by raising him to be the victor over death and the grave. And Easter is indeed the beautiful truth that our gracious God sent his son as the answer to our brokenness, our sinfulness, our humanness.

And for all of that, we who are gathered here this morning can be ever so grateful. Each one of us here has had our moments of darkness, our moments of pain, our times of brokenness when our hopes were dashed and our dreams destroyed, and we were left with what seemed to be an immovable stone. We have heard the doctor say words we didn't want to hear; we have anguished over words from our spouse, our children, our friends. We have watched what we had hoped would be a thriving business turn to ashes, and we have been assaulted by the throes of death itself. And the stone became heavier and buried our expectations for life even deeper.

Pain does happen. It is a part of life. And it leaves us numb. Sometimes facing a new morning is as tough a job as we think we can handle. Our lives get overrun with paying bills, looking after our children, facing April 15, wondering when the good weather is ever going to come.

And yet, in spite of all that, our gracious God sees us through. We only have to look around to those beside us to see an Easter story. I have been here long enough now to have seen many of you in times of crisis, and I have seen you hold fast to the resurrection hope that we celebrate here this Easter morning. Some of you will recognize yourselves and remember having said these words to me, "I don't know what I would have done without God to help me through." "What on earth do those people do who have no faith to cling to?" "I just knew that God was there with me, surrounding me with his love." "I have never done so much praying as I have in these last few months." And one last one I heard again just yesterday, "You know when you get to be my age, they say it is the golden years, but to me it seems like all I do is go to the funerals of my friends. I could never handle this without faith in the resurrection of Jesus." That is what Easter is all about. Easter is about faith. Easter is about hope. Easter is about the assurance that Jesus Christ did indeed die for our sins, and has set us free. And I don't know either how those who have no faith can cope. *I just don't know.*

And so, as we gather together here on this Easter morning, I want to remind you of some Scripture that goes beyond the promised rising of Jesus Christ, to our promised rising.

In John 5:24 Jesus says, "*Whoever hears my voice and believes in Him who sent me* will have eternal life and will not be condemned." Amen